Jane Goodall
A LIFE OF LOYALTY

by Kristin Sterling

Lerner Publications Company • Minneapolis

Photo Acknowledgments

The photographs in this book are used with the permission of: © Robyn Beck/AFP/Getty Images, cover; © Michael Nichols/National Geographic/Getty Images, p. 4; © Michael Nichols/National Geographic Society Image Collection, p. 6; © Thorsten Milse/Robert Harding World Imagery/Getty Images, p. 8; © John R. Kreul/Independent Picture Service, p. 9; © Three Lions/Hulton Archive/Getty Images, p. 10; The Jane Goodall Institute, p. 12; © Kennan Ward/CORBIS, p. 14; Hugo van Lawick/The Jane Goodall Institute, p. 16; © Paul Souders/CORBIS, p. 17; Bill Wallauer/The Jane Goodall Institute, p. 18; © age fotostock/SuperStock, p. 19; © Hugo van Lawick/National Geographic Society Image Collection, p. 20; © Peter Johnson/CORBIS, p. 22; © Karen Kasmauski/CORBIS, p. 23; © Bettmann/CORBIS, p. 24; © David S. Holloway/Getty Images, p. 25; AP Photo/Jean-Marc Bouju, p. 26.

Lerner Publications Company
A division of Lerner Publishing Group, Inc.
241 First Avenue North
Minneapolis, MN 55401 U.S.A.

Website address: www.lernerbooks.com

Words in **bold type** are explained in a glossary on page 31.

Library of Congress Cataloging-in-Publication Data

Sterling, Kristin.
    Jane Goodall : a life of loyalty / by Kristin Sterling.
        p.   cm. — (Pull ahead books—biographies)
    Includes index.
    ISBN 978-0-8225-8727-9 (lib. bdg. : alk. paper)
    1. Goodall, Jane, 1934– —Juvenile literature. 2. Primatologists—Biography—Juvenile
literature. 3. Women primatologists—Biography—Juvenile literature. I. Title.
    QL31.G58S74 2008
    590.92—dc22 [B]   2007011701

Manufactured in the United States of America
1 2 3 4 5 6 – JR – 13 12 11 10 09 08

Table of Contents

Jane studies her favorite animals in their forest home.

A Loyal Scientist

Do you like learning about animals? Jane Goodall has been studying **chimpanzees** for more than 40 years. She has been **loyal** to the animals she loves.

Jane grew up in this house.

Curious Jane

Jane Goodall was born in Great Britain in 1934. She loved playing outside and watching animals. She was curious. She asked many questions about nature.

Jane liked to read stories about animals in **Africa**.

Leopards live in many areas of Africa.

Zebras live in grassy, flat parts of Africa.

She told her mother that one day she would study wild animals in Africa.

Women work on a farm in Kenya.

Jane Goes to Africa

Jane went to Africa when she was 23 years old. She visited a friend there. Her friend lived in a country called Kenya. Jane decided to stay in Kenya.

Jane met a scientist named Louis Leakey. They worked together at a **museum**.

Jane with Louis Leakey

Louis was interested in chimpanzees.
He wanted to learn how they acted in
the wild. No one knew much about
their life in the jungle.

Chimpanzees live among the trees at Gombe.

Jane of the Jungle

Louis and Jane talked about chimpanzees for months. One day, she told him she wanted to study chimps in the wild. Louis sent Jane to the Gombe Stream Reserve. Gombe is in a country called Tanzania. Jane moved there to begin her **research**.

Jane could watch chimps from a spot called the Peak.

No one had lived near the chimpanzees before. The chimps stayed far away from Jane at first.

Jane followed them at a distance. She got closer to them over time. Finally, they got used to her. Then Jane could study their **behavior**.

Jane learned that chimps tease one another and play, as people do.

One day, she saw a chimp using a piece of grass as a **tool**. It used the grass to catch bugs to eat. Scientists had thought only people used tools.

Sometimes chimpanzees eat bushpigs.

Jane also learned that chimpanzees
hunt for meat. Most scientists thought
chimps ate only plants.

Jane with a baby chimp named Flint

Fame for Jane

Jane spent many years watching the chimps. She gave them names. She loved them as family. Jane wrote books and made movies about them.

Jane learned that the chimpanzees were in danger. People cut down the forests where chimpanzees lived. Some people hunted the chimps.

People cut down trees to use the wood.

Like this monkey, some chimps are kept in cages in labs.

Scientists did **experiments** on chimpanzees in labs.

In 1985, Jane spoke at a National Press Club meeting.

Jane wanted to help the chimps. She began teaching groups of people about the dangers chimpanzees faced.

Jane continues to teach people how to protect chimpanzees.

A Life of Loyalty

Jane Goodall has been loyal to her chimpanzee friends. She has spent her life studying and protecting them. Do you want to be like Jane?

Jane Goodall Timeline

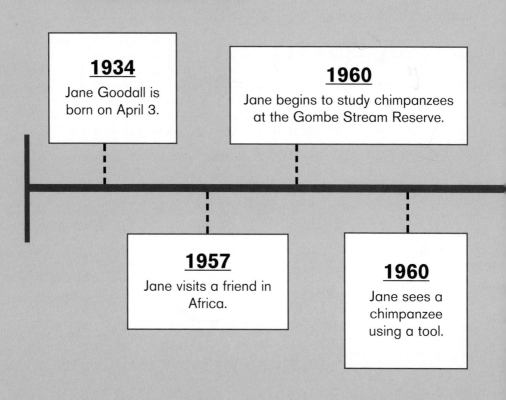

1934
Jane Goodall is born on April 3.

1960
Jane begins to study chimpanzees at the Gombe Stream Reserve.

1957
Jane visits a friend in Africa.

1960
Jane sees a chimpanzee using a tool.

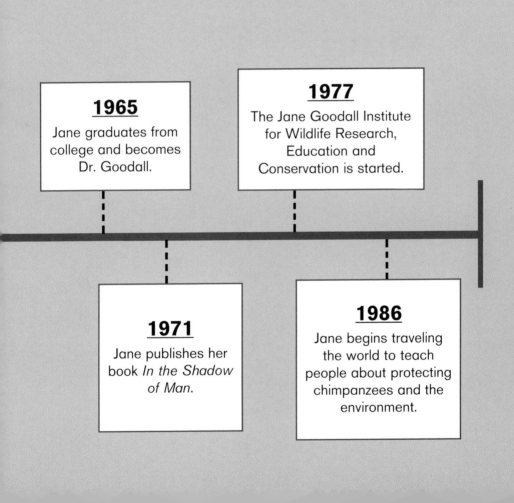

1965
Jane graduates from college and becomes Dr. Goodall.

1977
The Jane Goodall Institute for Wildlife Research, Education and Conservation is started.

1971
Jane publishes her book *In the Shadow of Man*.

1986
Jane begins traveling the world to teach people about protecting chimpanzees and the environment.

More about Jane Goodall

● Jane brought her mother, Vanne, with her when she started researching the chimps at Gombe.

● Jane is an ethologist. That is a person who studies the behavior of animals in their natural habitats.

● Jane has been married twice. She has one son.

● Jane has written several books for children.

Websites

ChimpanZoo
http://www.chimpanzoo.org

Jane Goodall Institute for Wildlife Research, Education and Conservation
http://www.janegoodall.org

Roots and Shoots
http://www.rootsandshoots.org

Glossary

Africa: one of Earth's seven continents. It is located south of Europe.

behavior: the way a living thing acts

chimpanzees: African apes with dark hair. They are also called chimps.

experiments: tests to find something out

loyal: faithful or devoted to someone or to a cause

museum: a building where people can see and learn about interesting objects

research: careful study

tool: something that is used to help do work

Index